HAL•LEONARD®
RECORDER SONGBOOK

FAVORITE MOVIE THEMES
2ND EDITION

T0061016

ISBN 978-0-7935-9193-0

HAL•LEONARD®
CORPORATION

7777 W. BLUEMOUND RD. P.O. BOX 13819 MILWAUKEE, WI 53213

Visit Hal Leonard Online at
www.halleonard.com

CHARIOTS OF FIRE

from CHARIOTS OF FIRE

Recorder

By VANGELIS

DANCING QUEEN

from MAMMA MIA!

RECORDER

Words and Music by BENNY ANDERSSON,
BJÖRN ULVAEUS and STIG ANDERSON

Strong Rock

small notes optional

DAWN
from PRIDE AND PREJUDICE

By DARIO MARIANELLI

RECORDER

FORREST GUMP – MAIN TITLE

(Feather Theme)

from the Paramount Motion Picture FORREST GUMP

RECORDER

Music by ALAN SILVESTRI

HE'S A PIRATE

from Walt Disney Pictures' PIRATES OF THE CARIBBEAN: THE CURSE OF THE BLACK PEARL

RECORDER

Music by KLAUS BADELT

I'M A BELIEVER

featured in the Dreamworks Motion Picture SHREK

RECORDER

Words and Music by
NEIL DIAMOND

IT WILL RAIN

from the Summit Entertainment film THE TWILIGHT SAGA: BREAKING DAWN - PART 1

RECORDER

Words and Music by BRUNO MARS,
PHILIP LAWRENCE and ARI LEVINE

THE JOHN DUNBAR THEME

from DANCES WITH WOLVES

RECORDER

By JOHN BARRY

THEME FROM "JURASSIC PARK"

from the Universal Motion Picture JURASSIC PARK

RECORDER

Composed by JOHN WILLIAMS

THE MAN FROM SNOWY RIVER
(Main Title Theme)
from THE MAN FROM SNOWY RIVER

RECORDER

By BRUCE ROWLAND

MISSION: IMPOSSIBLE THEME

from the Paramount Motion Picture MISSION: IMPOSSIBLE

RECORDER

By LALO SCHIFRIN

MY HEART WILL GO ON
(Love Theme from 'Titanic')
from the Paramount and Twentieth Century Fox Motion Picture TITANIC

RECORDER

Music by JAMES HORNER
Lyric by WILL JENNINGS

STAR TREK® THE MOTION PICTURE

Theme from the Paramount Picture STAR TREK: THE MOTION PICTURE

RECORDER

Music by JERRY GOLDSMITH

TEARS IN HEAVEN

featured in the Motion Picture RUSH

RECORDER

Words and Music by ERIC CLAPTON
and WILL JENNINGS